OUR GLOBAL
GREENHOUSE

OUR GLOBAL GREENHOUSE

BY APRIL KORAL
FRANKLIN WATTS A FIRST BOOK 1989
NEW YORK LONDON TORONTO SYDNEY

Cover photograph courtesy of: Magnum Photos

Photographs courtesy of:
Magnum Photos: pp. 8 (Dennis Stock), 11 (Erich
Hartmann), 20 (Martin J. Dain), 27 (Erich Hartmann),
32 (Philip J. Griffiths), 36 (bottom, Steve McCurry),
45 (Alex Webb), 49 (M. Bar'am), 53 (Sebastiao Salgado),
55 (Rene Burri); Black Starr: pp. 11 (Jay Lurie), 21
(Dennis Brack), 28 (Shelly Katz), 36 (top, James A.
Sugar); Stephen C. Delaney: p. 15; EPA-Documerica: p.
17; NOAA: p. 23; Photo Researchers: p. 24 (S. E.
Cornelius); Yellowstone National Park: p. 33; SERI:
p. 43; Associated Press: p. 44.

Library of Congress Cataloging-in-Publication Data

Koral, April.
Our global greenhouse / by April Koral.
p.   cm.—(A First book)
Includes index.
Summary: Discusses the origins, possible results,
and prevention of the environmental problem known
as the greenhouse effect.
ISBN 0-531-10745-0
1. Greenhouse effect. Atmospheric—Juvenile literature.
[1. Greenhouse effect. Atmospheric.] I. Title. II. Series.
QC912.3.K67 1989
363.73'92—dc20   89-8975   CIP   AC

To Judy and Margaret

CONTENTS

**THE GLASS WALLS AND ROOF
OF A GREENHOUSE HOLD
IN THE SUN-WARMED AIR.**

ONE
THE DELICATE
BALANCE

Greenhouses can be found in botanical gardens and plant nurseries. They are used to grow flowers, plants, fruits, and vegetables. The roof of a greenhouse is made of glass. So are the sides.

If you've ever been in a greenhouse, what you probably remember most about it was how warm it was. The reason the air is so warm inside a greenhouse is that the glass lets the heat from the sun in, but prevents most of the heat from escaping back out. The heat trapped inside is used to help grow plants that thrive in warm climates.

Like a greenhouse, the earth is warmed by the sun. Sunlight striking the surface of the earth is converted to *infrared*—heat—*radiation*. Most of this heat escapes back into space. But today more of it is being trapped in the earth's atmosphere. Because of the resemblance to the way heat is trapped in a greenhouse, scientists call this trend toward increased global warming the *greenhouse effect*.

The earth's average temperature has only rarely gone up or down more than three or four degrees Fahrenheit in the last ten thousand years. But scientists say that because of the greenhouse effect, our weather may change more in the next decade than it has in tens of thousands of years.

They predict that the earth will become hotter. In some parts of the world, winters will be warmer, while summers will be hotter. There will be more rainfall in the tropics of South America and Southeast Asia, where it already rains a great deal. In other places, such as in Egypt and areas of Africa where people often go hungry because there is not enough water to grow food, there may be even less rain.

The greenhouse effect will probably also change the weather of the United States. In Iowa, for example, there may no longer be enough rain to grow corn, and in Dallas the temperature might soar to over 100 degrees Fahrenheit (38° C) for seventy-eight days a year, instead of the nineteen days it now hits the 100 degree mark.

WHEN SUNLIGHT REACHES THE EARTH, IT IS CONVERTED TO HEAT. INSET: CORN GROWERS IN IOWA, ALONG WITH FARMERS EVERYWHERE, NEED ENOUGH RAIN FOR THEIR CROPS.

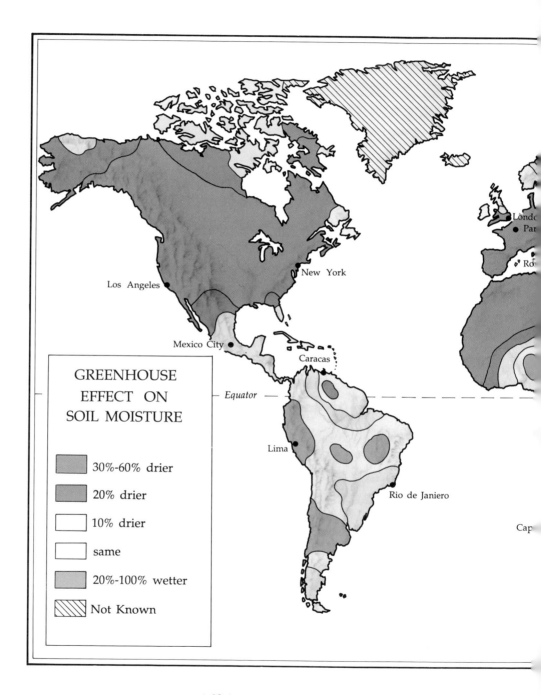

GREENHOUSE
EFFECT ON
SOIL MOISTURE

30%-60% drier

20% drier

10% drier

same

20%-100% wetter

Not Known

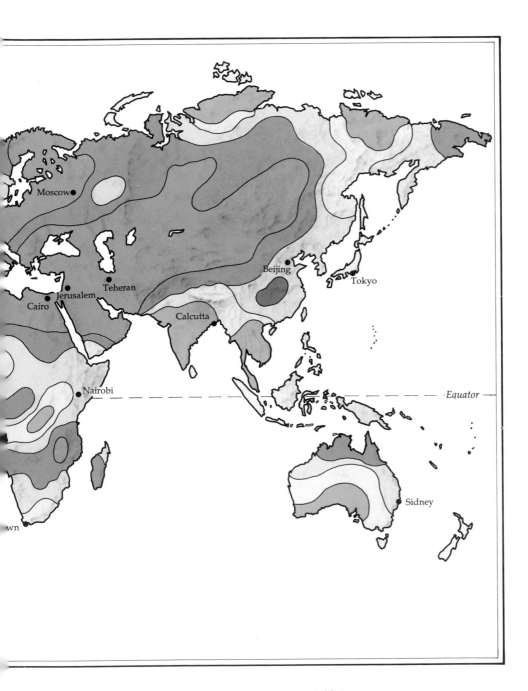

Moscow

Jerusalem
Cairo
Teheran
Calcutta

Beijing
Tokyo

Nairobi

Equator

Sidney

wn

Another possible result of the greenhouse effect will be that the world's oceans will rise, probably by 1 to 4 feet (0.3 to 1.2 m) during the next century. As the oceans rise, levels of salt in inland and underground waterways will increase, endangering freshwater fish and contaminating drinking supplies. Beaches and ports may be washed away by the water. Along the coasts of Louisiana, Texas, and Florida, many people might have to move from their homes.

A few scientists believe that some of these changes have already begun. We have been keeping temperature records for a hundred years or so. Four of the last ten years have been the hottest since recordkeeping began. And 1988 was the warmest year of all.

Why is this happening?

Our planet is a delicate balance of natural forces. It is like a wonderfully designed clock that never needs to be rewound or have its battery changed. It should just keep on ticking—unless we disturb the balance. This is what scientists say has been happening. We have been disturbing the balance of gases in the earth's atmosphere.

The *atmosphere* is the blanket of air that surrounds the earth and protects us from the sun's harshest rays. It contains mostly nitrogen (about 80 percent by volume) and oxygen (about 20 percent). There are also small amounts of many other gases. One of these gases is *carbon dioxide.*

**THE SKY SEEMS BEAUTIFUL, BUT THE PROBLEMS
ON THE EARTH REACH INTO THE ATMOSPHERE, TOO.**

Carbon dioxide plays an important role in living things. Animals and people breathe in oxygen and use it for energy and growth. Carbon dioxide is created in the process and breathed out as a waste product. Plants take in this carbon dioxide and make food with it, through the process of *photosynthesis.* They give off oxygen as a waste product. This is the oxygen we breathe in.

The amount of carbon dioxide in a planet's atmosphere affects the temperature on that planet. The earth has just the right amount of carbon dioxide in its atmosphere for life to thrive. In most parts of the planet, it is not too hot or too cold, and humans can live quite comfortably and raise food to eat.

Carbon dioxide exists naturally in the atmosphere in small quantities. But it is also produced every time we burn something that contains carbon. Carbon is in the so-called *fossil fuels*—coal, oil, and natural gas. We use these fossil fuels all the time—to run factories, power plants (which make electricity), cars, trucks, and buses. We also use them to heat our homes. Each time we burn a fossil fuel, more and more carbon dioxide floats up into the atmosphere. Right now the people of the world are putting more than 5.5 billion tons of carbon, in the form of carbon dioxide gas, into the atmosphere every year! Seventy-five percent of this amount comes from the burning of fossil fuels. The destruction of forests (see Chapter 2) accounts for most of the rest. As more and more carbon dioxide builds up in

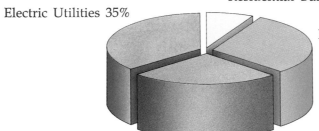

SOURCES OF CARBON DIOXIDE

Percent of U.S. Carbon Dioxide emissions in 1987
Source: World Resources Institute

Electric Utilities 35%

Residential Buildings 11%

Industry 24%

Transportation 30%

the atmosphere, less heat can escape, and the planet gets hotter.

Other gases are also trapping the planet's heat. These include CFCs (see Chapter 2), methane, and nitrous oxide. Like carbon dioxide, some of these other greenhouse gases, including methane and nitrous oxide, have been in our planet's atmosphere for a long time. But we are now producing them in much larger amounts than ever before. Others, such as CFCs, are relatively new and made only in factories and laboratories.

This tremendous increase in the quantities of greenhouse gases has upset the atmosphere's delicate balance. The result may be the most serious environmental problem this planet has ever faced. How did it happen?

TWO
OUR CHANGING
WORLD

Imagine what life must have been like for your great-great grandparents. To cool off during the summer, they might have sat out on their front porch. If they lived in the city, they might have slept on the fire escape in the hope of catching a breeze. To keep food cold and fresh, they probably bought ice from a man who sold it on the street. And if they were like many Americans who lived in the early 1900s, they grew much of their own food and made their own clothing—sewing at night by the light of a candle or a small lamp lit with gas.

Our lives today are very different. In the summertime most Americans shop in air-conditioned stores and work in air-conditioned offices. Thousands of factories around the country—and world—make our clothing, furniture, toys, and nearly everything else that we use. Big power plants supply electricity, which we use every time we switch on the light, make toast, or heat something up in the micro-wave oven.

POWER LINES CARRY ELECTRICITY FROM GIANT PLANTS TO HOMES, FACTORIES, AND STORES EVERYWHERE. FACING PAGE: THE EXHAUST FUMES FROM CARS CONTAIN NITROUS OXIDE, ONE OF THE GREENHOUSE GASES.

To run our factories, we need energy, mostly in the form of electricity. To heat our homes, we need energy. And to run our cars, we also need energy. We get most of our energy by burning coal, oil, or gas. And, as you now know, every time we burn one of these fossil fuels, we release carbon dioxide gas, which contributes to the greenhouse effect.

Some scientists have been concerned for a long time about what might happen if there was too much carbon dioxide in our atmosphere. In 1861 a British scientist did an experiment showing that carbon dioxide absorbed some of the infrared radiation, or heat, that the earth naturally would have reflected into space. Soon afterward a Swedish scientist claimed that if the amount of carbon dioxide in the atmosphere doubled, enough infrared radiation would be trapped to increase the average temperature of the earth by several degrees.

But these scientists were lonely voices, and no one paid much attention to them. Then, in 1988, James Hansen, a respected scientist working at the National Aeronautics and Space Administration Goddard Institute for Space Studies in New York City told Congress during special hearings that it was "a fact" that greenhouse gases were increasing, that the earth was getting warmer, and that "the greenhouse effect is occurring now and it is changing global climate." Other scientists who agreed with Dr. Hansen's conclusions also spoke at the hearings. As these experts gave their testimony, a record-breaking heat wave was beginning to spread across the country. Suddenly, government leaders and the public became very interested in the danger of too much carbon dioxide and other greenhouse gases in the atmosphere.

It is estimated that since the Industrial Revolution began in the mid-1800s and people began building many

SCIENTISTS AT AN OBSERVATORY IN BOULDER, COLORADO, SEND UP A BALLOON TO MEASURE GREENHOUSE GASES.

factories and burning large quantities of fossil fuels, there has been nearly a 25 percent increase in carbon dioxide in the atmosphere. How do scientists know this? They measure carbon dioxide in the air that became trapped in glaciers (slow-moving large bodies of ice) hundreds of years ago. They then compare this to the amounts of carbon dioxide in samples of today's air. Measurements of today's air are taken at the Mauna Loa Observatory in Hawaii as well as at more remote locations such as Point Barrow, Alaska, and Antarctica.

Up until recently about half of the carbon dioxide that we produced was absorbed by the world's trees and oceans. The rest remained in the atmosphere.

Unfortunately, we are not only producing more carbon dioxide but our world is also absorbing less of it. That's because there are fewer trees than before. All around the planet forests are being destroyed. Farmers cut down trees to plant more crops or open up space to raise cattle for beef. As much as 100 acres (40 ha) of the world's remaining forests are being destroyed every minute every day of the year!

In addition, burning wood adds carbon dioxide to the air. Some scientists say that the millions of trees being burned every year in the rain forests of Brazil may be responsible for one-tenth of the carbon dioxide added each year to the atmosphere. According to some estimates, due to its massive tree-clearing efforts, Brazil currently ranks third in carbon dioxide emissions.

MILLIONS OF TREES AROUND THE WORLD ARE BEING DESTROYED. THIS FOREST IN HONDURAS IS BEING CUT DOWN.

In the United States and Europe, forests are also disappearing due to pollution from coal-burning power plants. Winds carry the pollution from one state to another. A forest in New York, for example, may be affected by power plants operating as far away as Ohio.

Carbon dioxide is just one of the gases that is causing the greenhouse effect. Other greenhouse gases are also the by-products of our changing world.

When we want to get a quick meal, we stop in a fast-food restaurant and get a hamburger. No one washes the plastic container it is served in. We just throw it away. The container is usually made with *CFCs* (short for *chloro-fluorocarbons*), a material invented by researchers in the 1930s. Like carbon dioxide, CFCs absorb infrared radiation and make our planet warmer. CFCs are also used to make aerosol spray cans, refrigerants, air conditioners, the foam in car seats, and to clean electronic equipment. In the late 1970s, the United States, Canada, Sweden, and Norway banned the use of aerosols that were made with CFCs. After the ban, manufacturers used another method they had developed to make spray come out of cans. Unfortunately, CFCs are still used to make spray cans in other countries.

CFCs have a long lifetime. Even after you have thrown away the plastic container from the fast-food restaurant or tossed an old refrigerator in the dump, the CFCs do not disappear. In fact, they may stay in the atmosphere for as long as three hundred years! The United States and other

**COAL-BURNING POWER PLANTS
AND FACTORIES HAVE DAMAGED
THIS FOREST IN GERMANY.**

highly developed nations in the world are using more and more CFCs, and scientists believe they are to blame for up to 20 percent of the greenhouse effect.

Other dangerous greenhouse gases that trap the earth's heat are nitrous oxide and methane, which are produced by decaying vegetation, particularly in rice paddies, and by the use of chemical fertilizers, coal mining, and the burning of fossil fuels and wood. Tiny particles of methane stay in the atmosphere for only about ten years. But nitrous oxide particles linger for up to 170 years!

Although greenhouse gases can have a tremendous effect on our planet, they are only a small part of the atmosphere. If our atmosphere were the size of an average swimming pool, there would be about a barrel of carbon dioxide, 8 liters of methane, 30 teaspoons of nitrous oxide, and only 2 drops of CFCs.

But even a tiny increase in the amount of greenhouse gases in our atmosphere can result in a dramatic change in our climate—and our lives.

FAST-FOOD RESTAURANTS USE CONTAINERS MADE WITH CFCS.

THREE
LIVING IN A
GREENHOUSE

What will the world of the future be like if the greenhouse effect occurs the way scientists predict?

Some scientists say that our planet will warm up an average of 3 degrees Fahrenheit. Others say it will be as much as 9 degrees hotter by the year 2030. A range of 3 to 9 degrees might not seem like that much, but even a 3-degree warming would have a dramatic effect on our world.

In the summer of 1988, when temperatures in the United States were over 90 degrees Fahrenheit (33° C) for weeks, the weather was on the front page of newspapers nearly every day. In Detroit, automobile workers were sent home because it was too hot to work in the factories. Restaurants and stores without air-conditioning lost most of their customers. Some people, especially the elderly, became sick and even died from the heat.

The hotter it got, the more people wanted to use their

air conditioners. Office buildings and malls that have no windows had to be air-conditioned all the time. There was no other way to cool the air inside. But it takes electricity to run air conditioners, and our power plants are able to make only a certain amount of electricity.

Sometimes the demand for electrical power during the heat wave of 1988 was too great. In several cities the power plants had to "borrow" electricity from neighboring states or Canada. To avoid a complete blackout, power was drastically reduced or cut off in certain parts of New York City for a few days. Otherwise the whole city might have been without lights and the electric energy to run air conditioners, refrigerators, and elevators.

If the world becomes hotter, summers like this would be typical, with heat waves that might last even longer. More people would suffer.

In some places there might be less rain, too. Farmers in dozens of states would discover that there was too little rain to grow wheat, corn, and other essential crops. As it became harder to raise food, prices for that food would undoubtedly go up.

There would be even less rain in some parts of the West and Southwest. In some of these areas there have already been water shortages due to drought. Several of the states in these regions have recently passed laws limiting how often you can water your garden and forbidding restaurants

WITHOUT ENOUGH RAIN, THE CORN PLANTED
IN THIS NORTH DAKOTA FIELD CAN'T GROW.
FACING PAGE: HEAT AND LACK OF RAIN
CAN MEAN MORE TERRIBLE FOREST FIRES,
SUCH AS THIS ONE THAT RAGED THROUGH
YELLOWSTONE NATIONAL PARK IN 1988.

to serve water unless a customer asks for it. In a green-house world will these states have enough water for people to drink?

During the extended heat wave of 1988, the nation's forests became drier and drier. Fires that started in Yellow-stone National Park spread quickly. Forest rangers thought at first that the fires would burn themselves out before doing extensive damage. But, partly due to the drought and unusually hot conditions, they didn't. By the end of the summer, about 20 percent of the park's trees had burned down. Forest rangers estimate that it will take sixty to one hundred years for new trees to grow to the height of the ones that were destroyed.

On the other side of the globe, in Asia, less rain will mean that farmers may not be able to grow enough rice, which requires a lot of water. Sixty percent of the world's people depend on rice as the main part of their diet. If they don't have enough rice, what will they eat? Most poor countries do not have extra supplies of food stored away for when their farmers cannot grow enough food for their people. Nor do they have the money to buy food from other countries, even if it is available.

Some areas of the world will probably get more rain. A warmer, wetter climate would help the farmers of central Europe grow more wheat. In Finland, which usually has long, very cold winters, the greenhouse effect would mean being able to grow more barley. But in Canada, more rain could mean losing a quarter of the country's wheat crop. And for farmers all over the world, too much rain means an increase in the number of insects that carry disease and kill plants.

Scientists predict that the greenhouse effect will help some plants to grow bigger. That's because carbon dioxide, which is the main greenhouse gas, is a natural fertilizer. Plants grown in special laboratories where there is a lot of carbon dioxide in the air not only grow larger but need less water. An increase in carbon dioxide in the air, however, will mean that weeds may grow bigger, too!

As temperatures increase, the world will change in other ways. Scientists say that the oceans may rise by 1 foot (0.3 m) in the next forty years or so, and 2 to 4 feet (0.7 to 1.3 m) in the next hundred years. The reason for this is that ocean water expands—that is, increases in volume—as it gets warmer. Snow from mountaintops and even the ice covering the North Pole could melt and make the oceans rise even more.

What would happen if the level of the sea rose? Nearly one-third of all human beings live within 40 miles (64 km) of a coastline. In the United States and elsewhere, many cities and homes are built near the ocean. These areas could be flooded by the rising waters. Beaches could become covered by water, and some ports and bridges might be destroyed.

The rising waters would do more damage to some

countries than to others. A 6-foot (1.8-m) rise in water would flood 20 percent of the Asian nation of Bangladesh, for example. Rich countries might be able to build walls to protect themselves from the sea, but what would poor nations do?

Scientists are increasingly concerned about a particularly dangerous effect of the CFCs. This greenhouse gas does more than just contribute to the warming of the planet. Researchers are now finding out that CFCs can harm the earth in other ways.

In 1987 scientists from the United States and other nations sent two airplanes on an unusual voyage. The planes went 65,000 feet (20,000 m) up to investigate a "hole" in the sky over the Antarctic that had been detected earlier by satellites and computers. The "hole" isn't exactly

ABOVE: IF THE SEA LEVEL
RISES, SHORELINE HOMES —
SUCH AS THESE FLOODED BY
STORMS AND HIGH TIDES IN
VIRGINIA BEACH, VIRGINIA —
WOULD BE IN GREAT DANGER.
BELOW: PARTS OF THE WORLD
ALREADY HAVE HEAVY RAINY
SEASONS. MORE RAIN WOULD
DAMAGE THE CROPS OF THIS
FARMER IN NEPAL.

**THE BLANKET OF AIR
SURROUNDING THE EARTH
PROTECTS IT FROM THE SUN.**

a hole. It is a section of sky where the atmosphere seems to be thinning out. The area where this is happening is not small. In fact, it is as large as the United States!

Why is this happening to the atmosphere? Is it a natural occurrence or caused by industrial pollution? The part of the atmosphere the hole is in is called the *ozone layer*. Scientists believe that the ozone layer is slowly being broken down by CFCs. Just one CFC particle can break down tens of thousands of ozone particles.

Although the ozone layer is made up mostly of other gases, it is the ozone that shields us from much of the sun's ultraviolet rays and prevents them from reaching the surface of the earth. Too many ultraviolet rays can cause cataracts, a serious eye condition, and skin cancer. Skin cancer has been on the rise. Scientists predict that if the ozone layer continues to be eaten away, millions more people will develop it. The excess rays may also impair the body's immune system, which fights disease.

Experts are also concerned about the effect of excessive ultraviolet rays on plants and animals. Scientists fear that the ultraviolet light will damage phytoplankton, tiny one-celled plants that float near the top of the ocean. Many fish depend on these plants to survive. In addition, phytoplankton take in vast amounts of carbon dioxide. If they die, carbon dioxide levels could get even higher and speed up the global warming process.

Because of the increase in greenhouse gases, the earth may face many serious problems. The question now is, how do we solve them? Or better yet, how do we prevent them from happening in the first place?

FOUR
THE DEBATE:
WHAT TO
DO?

People often disagree with each other, whether it is children in a playground or scientists trying to solve a difficult problem. Experts who have studied the greenhouse effect, for example, do not agree on what we should do about this serious threat to our planet.

Some scientists say that in order to stop or even slow down the warming of our planet, we must take dramatic and quick action. Such actions may mean sacrifices on the part of Americans and others around the world. They will also be expensive to implement.

Other scientists, though these are now a minority, say that we do not need to rush into action. Perhaps nature will somehow restore the delicate balance and set things right. Perhaps the oceans will absorb more of the carbon dioxide, or more clouds will form to protect us from the sun's dangerous rays. Besides, these scientists say, we don't have enough proof that the greenhouse effect will be so bad.

Finally, still other scientists say that it may be too late to prevent the greenhouse effect. We must simply prepare for its coming.

Scientific conclusions are usually based on concrete experiments conducted in the laboratory. There, researchers carefully observe and analyze the results of their tests. But scientists cannot do the same kinds of tests when they are trying to predict possible *future* occurrences. They cannot add more carbon dioxide to the earth's atmosphere to see what will happen. They cannot raise the earth's temperature to see how much the oceans will rise.

What, then, is the laboratory of scientists who study the greenhouse effect? It is a room filled with powerful computers. To make a prediction about our future climate, researchers take into account how much coal, oil, and gas is likely to be used, how much the population will grow, and how many more factories there will be producing goods. They also feed into the computer facts we already know about our weather, oceans, and rainfall as well as thousands of other pieces of information about the way our planet works. With these and other data, the computer is able to make predictions about what the climate of the world will be like at some future time.

Of course, how accurate these predictions are depends on the quality of the information fed into the computer. Can we be sure how many factories will be built in the future?

Do we really know how much fossil fuel will be burned? Exactly how much more heat will be trapped if the quantities of greenhouse gases increase?

Although some scientists question how *much* warmer our planet will get, most experts agree that at least some warming will happen. Indeed, they believe there is nothing we can do now to prevent the temperature from rising by at least three degrees Fahrenheit by the year 2020. The best we can do, these experts say, is not to let it get dangerously warmer. And that means changing the way we live *now*.

Even if we were to begin taking steps today to cut down on greenhouse gases, we would have to wait at least another twenty to thirty years to see a change in our atmosphere. That's why it's important to start now. What are some of these first steps that we can begin to take?

To start, we must find sources of energy other than coal, oil, and gas. Many people say that the government should help support research programs exploring alternatives. They say that finding alternate energy sources that are economical to use is as urgent as finding a cure for AIDS or other serious diseases.

We already know other ways to obtain energy. In fact, one of the best sources of energy is right above our heads— the sun. We have only begun to harness the sun's rays to produce electricity. Throughout the United States people have built homes with solar panels on the roof; they warm the house and provide hot water. Several companies in the

**SOLAR PANELS CAPTURE THE
POWER OF THE SUN AND CONVERT
IT INTO ELECTRICITY.**

United States have built power plants that are run by the
sun's energy. One day we may be using this energy even
more, but right now it is still a very costly alternative. Other
alternative energy sources include hydropower (electricity
from running water), wind power, and possibly—in the
future—fusion (the way the sun produces energy, by com-
bining atoms).

Other people believe we should be building more nuclear power plants. One nuclear power plant can provide electricity to hundreds of thousands of homes—and produces no harmful greenhouse gases. But there are dangers in using nuclear power, which is the splitting of atoms to release energy. In the spring of 1986, for example, in Chernobyl in the Soviet Union, there was an accident in a nuclear power plant resulting in an explosion that sent a radioactive cloud into the surrounding atmosphere.

The consequences of the accident were sobering. Over 100,000 people from the city of Chernobyl and nearby towns had to be evacuated from their homes. In the next few weeks, the radioactive cloud traveled north and west from Chernobyl, depositing its deadly cargo across parts of

NUCLEAR POWER PLANTS CAN PRODUCE A GREAT DEAL OF ENERGY, BUT MANY PEOPLE ARE CONCERNED ABOUT THE RISKS THEY POSE. INSET: AFTER THE CHERNOBYL ACCIDENT, NEARBY VILLAGES WERE EMPTIED AND PEOPLE WHO LIVED AT GREATER DISTANCES WERE CHECKED FOR EXPOSURE TO RADIATION.

Europe. There was even a small increase in radioactivity in California. Throughout Europe fruits, vegetables, butter, milk, and other foodstuffs had to be destroyed because they were contaminated. The towns right near the nuclear power plant in the USSR had to be razed by bulldozers. No one will be able to live there for decades, perhaps even longer. Twenty-nine firefighters died from the radiation poisoning they received while fighting the fires at the plant. And thousands of people around the world are projected to develop cancer one day as a result of being exposed to radiation from Chernobyl.

Because of this nuclear accident and one in Harrisburg, Pennsylvania, in 1979, as well as the high costs of building safe nuclear power plants and the difficulties in disposing of the spent fuel (which is radioactive and will remain so for many years), there are no new power plants currently being built in the United States. However, as a result of recent fears concerning the greenhouse effect, those who favor nuclear energy have begun to push for the building of more nuclear power plants.

Scientists note that there is something all of us can do right now to slow down the greenhouse effect—we can start *conserving*—saving—energy. We can insulate our homes better so that less heat is needed to warm them in the winter. We can use less air conditioning during the summer. Consumers can buy cars that use less gasoline and car manufacturers can be required to produce far more energy-

**AN OKLAHOMA TEACHER'S COMPRESSED-
AIR CAR CONSERVES ENERGY, BUT IT IS
NOT BEING PRODUCED.**

efficient cars. Some scientists are working on developing powerful electrical batteries that can be used instead of gasoline to run cars. A high school science teacher in Oklahoma invented a car that ran on compressed air, but none of the car manufacturers were interested in producing it!

We could also use more efficient light bulbs and electrical appliances. Our air conditioners and refrigerators could easily be redesigned so that the coolants, which contain the deadly CFCs, could be removed before the appliances are crushed in the junkyard, thereby preventing the CFCs from being released into the atmosphere.

Experts also point out that many products can be made using substitutes for CFCs. Some substitutes are already available, and others are being developed. And all countries around the world can begin a campaign to plant millions of trees that would absorb large amounts of carbon dioxide.

No matter what steps we take, however, there will probably be some global warming. Thus, we may have to start preparing ourselves in practical ways. In low-lying areas, for example, walls can be built to stop the ocean from swallowing up beaches and nearby houses and ports. In Holland walls called dikes have been holding back the ocean for centuries.

We can also begin to cultivate seeds that need less water to grow, or learn to use the water we have more efficiently. In Israel, for example, farmers have discovered ways to grow vegetables in the middle of the desert, where there is very little rain.

Some scientists have made other, more radical suggestions on how we might deal with the greenhouse effect. Nobody knows if any of them will work. Some of these rather imaginative ideas include sending blimps carrying ozone into the atmosphere to replace lost ozone; shooting laser beams into the sky to blast apart CFCs; fertilizing the

IN ISRAEL, AGRICULTURALISTS DEVELOP
TECHNIQUES AND SEEDS THAT ARE BETTER
SUITED TO DESERT FARMING.

oceans to increase the number of living organisms that can absorb carbon dioxide; and building solar power satellites that would collect solar energy and beam electricity back to earth. Another suggestion has been to trap the carbon dioxide emitted by smokestacks and transport it to the middle of the ocean, where it can be dumped.

There are many steps that we, in the United States, can take to protect our planet. Unfortunately, we may not take any of them. People have their own special interests, and these interests are often in conflict with national or global interests. Some companies will not voluntarily limit the amount of coal or oil their factories burn, or they refuse to put in expensive "scrubbers" that can reduce the amount of carbon dioxide released by their plants. In states where coal is mined, some people do not want coal-mining companies to close down. They are afraid of losing their jobs. How will they make a living?

How, then, can we begin to fight the greenhouse effect? The best way is for the nations of the world to work together. Although we speak different languages and have different customs, we all breathe in the same atmosphere as it circulates around the globe. How can we work together to save it?

FIVE
WORKING
TOGETHER AS
A PLANET

Every day, in many parts of the world, there are countries at war. Rarely do the leaders of these nations work hard at finding a peaceful solution. Now there is a war that all nations must fight, but they must fight it together. It is a war to save our planet.

Why is it so important that all countries work together? Because greenhouse gases do not recognize borders between countries. The carbon dioxide that comes out of smokestacks in factories in China enters the atmosphere—the same atmosphere that Americans, Italians, Greeks, Africans, and everyone else living on this planet shares. It does little good if one country bans CFCs and another country does not.

Who is most responsible for the greenhouse effect? The wealthiest and most developed nations. The United States leads the world in fossil-fuel emissions, at about 25 percent of the total; the USSR and China together contribute about 33 percent; and the nations of Western Europe and Japan together contribute about 23 percent. Some experts claim that the United States, with only 5 percent of the world's population, is responsible for roughly 20 percent of the entire global greenhouse effect.

Can these countries work together with others to prevent or slow down the greenhouse effect? Are all the countries involved willing to set limits on the amounts of greenhouse gases they produce?

Very slowly some countries have begun to do just that.

In 1987 some forty nations, including the United States, met in Montreal, Canada, to discuss an agreement that would reduce the amount of CFCs in the atmosphere. The Montreal Protocol, as the agreement is called, took ten years to negotiate! The treaty, which has been signed thus far by thirty-seven countries, was prompted mainly by reports of a "hole," believed to be caused by CFCs, in the ozone layer over Antarctica. Countries who signed the protocol agreed, as of 1990, to freeze CFC production at 1986 levels and to cut back on CFC production by another 50 percent by 1998. Then, in March 1989, twelve European countries agreed to completely end the production of certain CFCs by the year 2000.

In June 1988 the World Conference on the Changing Atmosphere was held in Toronto. In attendance were scientists from around the world who are especially concerned with the issue of global warming. They called for a 20 percent cut in world carbon dioxide emissions. And in

AS NATIONS BUILD POWER PLANTS TO IMPROVE
THEIR STANDARDS OF LIVING, THEY ALSO BUILD UP
POLLUTION, AS HERE IN CUBATAO, BRAZIL.

November 1988 representatives from thirty-five nations met in Geneva, Switzerland, for three days to discuss global warming and set up groups to study various aspects of the problem.

Already, though, many scientists are saying that the Montreal Protocol treaty does not reduce the level of CFCs enough. They ask why the countries didn't agree to ban the production of this dangerous chemical completely.

There are additional signs that countries are willing to work together. The United States and the Soviet Union have begun a program in which scientists from each country can "talk" to each other over their computer terminals and exchange information about greenhouse gases.

Most countries agree that, to reduce greenhouse gases, we must do more than just talk to each other and exchange information. We must begin to pass laws to control the production of these gases that everyone on the planet will obey. But is this fair?

The greenhouse gases are often the by-products of the things that have made our lives easier. They come from the factories that turn out our cars and clothing, and energy plants that produce electricity. The poorer nations of the world are very anxious to build more power plants and to be able to produce more goods for their people. They don't think that it is right that the richer countries of the world, who are largely responsible for the greenhouse effect, should now tell them what they can and cannot do. "Your

AS CHINA INDUSTRIALIZES, AND
CARS REPLACE BICYCLES, ENORMOUS
AMOUNTS OF COAL AND OTHER FOSSIL
FUELS WILL BE BURNED.

citizens already own cars, live in comfortable houses, and have refrigerators," they say. "Why shouldn't ours?"

Furthermore, how could a ban on producing dangerous greenhouse gases be enforced? Who would be the police for the world?

One way to encourage cooperation, some people say, is for the wealthier nations who have lent money to other countries to cancel their debts. In return the less wealthy nations would agree to cut down on their production of greenhouse gases and take other steps to slow down the greenhouse effect. Bolivia and Costa Rica have recently agreed to set aside parks and preserve forests in exchange for not paying off their foreign debts. The richer nations of the world could also help by encouraging the development of economical alternate energy sources for use worldwide.

The last time the United States, Europe, and the Soviet Union worked together was in World War II, to fight a mad dictator from Germany who threatened the world. Now they must band together again. This fight, too, must be won, both for ourselves and for others who have not yet been born.

SIX
EXPLORING
ON YOUR
OWN

In this chapter we will present several simple ways in which you can learn more on your own about the greenhouse effect, through observation and experimentation.

Experiment #1:
Gases Can Travel

How do carbon dioxide and other greenhouse gases get into the atmosphere? Through a method called *diffusion*. The molecules—the tiny particles that make up the gases—travel from where there is a high concentration (many) of them to places where there is a lower concentration.

Here's an experiment to show that gas molecules travel and diffuse into the air.

Ask your mother if you can borrow a bottle of perfume or toilet water. Stand at one end of the hall while a friend stands at the other end with the bottle. Have your friend open the bottle. Your nose will tell you when the molecules of perfume have reached you. Do it again, and time how long it takes for you to detect the gas. Now you know how fast the molecules travel. Repeat the experiment with a bottle of vanilla. Does it take the same length of time?

Experiment #2:
Measuring Rain

Scientists say that rain will increase in some areas and decrease in others as a result of the greenhouse effect. They are talking about *average* rainfall. To find the average rainfall, they measure in different places. Be a scientist and measure how much rain falls in your hometown.

Find a tall flat-bottomed jar and put a funnel in it that fits the mouth of the jar. Put the jar outside, away from trees. After a rain measure the water by putting a ruler inside the jar. Write down the amount on a chart and then empty the jar. After the next rain, measure again and enter that amount on your chart. At the end of a month, add up the amount. How much did it rain in one month? Repeat your experiment the next month. Try again a few months later. Are some months rainier than others where you live?

Experiment #3:
Why Will the Oceans Rise?

There is a fear that ice from glaciers in remote places such as Greenland will melt if the temperature increases. What effect will this have on the world's oceans?

Put an ice cube in a glass. Now fill the glass to the top with water. Let the ice melt. Imagine that the water in the glass is the ocean. What will happen to the oceans? If they expand, where will the water go?

Experiment #4:
Building a Greenhouse

The effect of carbon dioxide and other gases on the atmosphere is called the greenhouse effect because the gases trap heat somewhat the way a greenhouse does. The glass lets sunlight enter but prevents some of the heat from escaping. Why don't you build your own model of a greenhouse? Ask your teacher or a parent to help you.

Take a sheet of plastic and cut a few small holes in it. Put a thermometer inside an empty fishtank. (This tank represents the earth.) What is the temperature inside the tank? Now cover the tank with the plastic, taping down the sides. Put the tank in the sun. Check the temperature of the tank after a few hours.

The holes in the plastic let some of the heat escape. Now put a new piece of plastic, with no holes in it, over the tank. This is like having a large quantity of greenhouse gases in the atmosphere. What effect does this have on the temperature of the tank? Do you see how too high a concentration of greenhouse gases could affect our planet's climate?

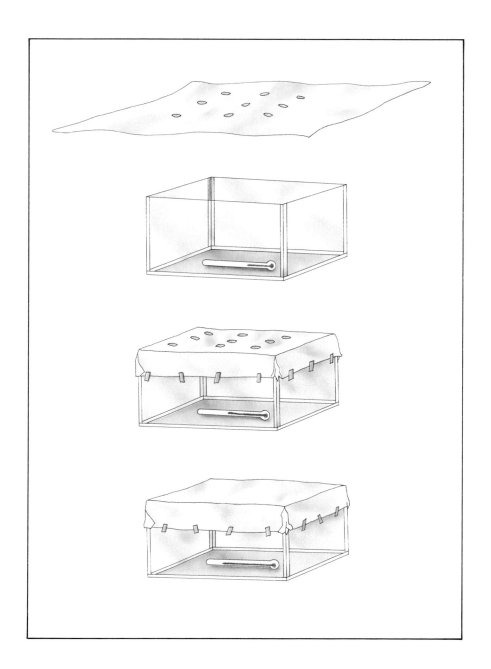

INDEX